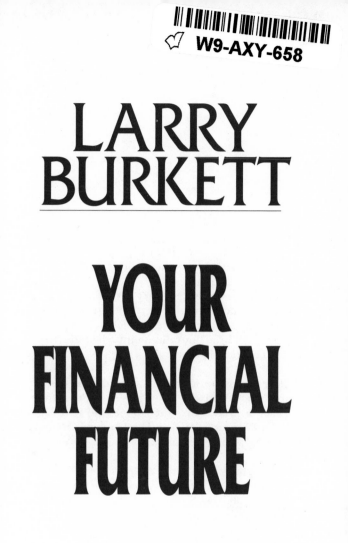

LARRY BURKETT

YOUR FINANCIAL FUTURE

MOODY PRESS
CHICAGO

© 1992 by
CHRISTIAN FINANCIAL CONCEPTS

All rights reserved. No part of this book may be reproduced in any form without permission in writing from the publisher, except in the case of brief quotations embodied in critical articles or reviews.

Scripture quotations, unless noted otherwise, are taken from the *New American Standard Bible*, © 1960, 1962, 1963, 1968, 1971, 1972, 1973, 1975, and 1977 by The Lockman Foundation. Used by permission.

The segment entitled "Widows Need Early Financial Training" has been reprinted by permission from Section 2 of *The Complete Financial Guide for Single Parents*, by Larry Burkett. Copyright 1991 by Scripture Press. Published by Victor Books.

ISBN: 0-8024-2608-5

1 2 3 4 5 6 Printing/VP/Year 96 95 94 93 92

Printed in the United States of America

About the Author

Larry Burkett is committed to teaching God's people His principles for managing money. Unfortunately, money management is one area often neglected by Christians, and it is a major cause of conflict and disruption in both business and family life.

For more than two decades Larry has counseled and taught God's principles for finance across the country. As president of Christian Financial Concepts, Larry has counseled, conducted seminars, and written numerous books on the subject of maintaining control of the budget. In additon he is heard on more than 1,000 radio outlets worldwide.

Retirement

To most people in our society, retirement refers to that period of time in our latter years when we can stop work and start enjoying life. This idea of retirement is very appealing. After all, we worked hard to get where we are, and we "deserve" the opportunity to enjoy it, don't we?

RETIREMENT FOR EVERYONE?

The truth of the matter is that although many people are geared to look forward to that kind of retirement, most of them do not have the means to actually do it. But, because we have bought into the concept that *everyone* should retire, we force our workers to retire prematurely and cause them to scrape by on inadequate pensions, Social Security, or even welfare. Do these people kick back and enjoy life? Hardly!

Obviously, not all retirement is wrong any more than all borrowing is wrong. It's a matter of degree. In some professions, such as athletics, age is a critical factor, and retirement is inevitable. In other professions, everyday stress eventually "burns a person out," making some sort of change highly advisable. And retirement does provide certain benefits to society:

1. The shift to a lesser income necessitates a more moderate lifestyle.

2. The goal of retirement creates savings that can be used to help build and create jobs for others.

A major problem develops, however, when we begin to say that everyone who reaches a certain age is no longer productive and must be replaced with more aggressive "youngsters." This concept is not only out of step with the historical record of the impressive accomplishments of countless elder statesmen, soldiers, philosophers, teachers, monarchs, and men and women of God, but also it cannot be supported scripturally.

Scriptural Retirement

The only reference in the Bible to retirement is found in Numbers 8:25: "But at the age of fifty years they shall retire from service in the work and not work any more." That's not much of a foundation to go on when building a multi-billion-dollar retirement system such as we have today, particularly since the temple priests referred to in this passage then took on other priestly duties.

Also consider the example of the apostle Paul. He had certainly served his time in the service of the Lord even before he began his third missionary journey. No one would have faulted him if he had elected to retire at Corinth or Ephesus and write his memoirs. He might even have returned to his Mediterranean home near the city of Tarsus and lived out his remaining years in peace. Yet, he chose to continue his journeys, giving no thought to retirement as long as he was able to perform the duties God assigned him. At that time, Paul was probably in his late sixties—ancient by the standards of his generation!

No, the normal system of "retirement" throughout God's Word is the *sabbatical*. The first sabbatical instituted was a day of rest each week called the Sabbath. Additionally, a Jew was required to let his land lie idle every seventh year. "Six years you shall sow your field, and six years you shall prune your vineyard and gather in its crop, but during the seventh year the land shall have a sabbath rest, a sabbath to the Lord; you shall not sow your field nor prune your vineyard" (Leviticus 25:3-4).

Wouldn't it be great to take retirement through sabbaticals? That would mean we would work six years and take the seventh off. That year could be utilized for continued education, missions work, new technology training, or simply to enjoy our families while we are still young.

PLANNING FOR RETIREMENT

Retirement planning in and of itself is not wrong. In fact, it exemplifies the kind of prudence commended by many verses in the Bible, including Proverbs 27:12, "A prudent man sees evil and hides himself, the naive proceed and pay the penalty."

In Proverbs 6:6-8 we are given the example of the ant: "Go to the ant, O sluggard, observe her ways and be wise, which having no chief, officer or ruler, prepares her food in the summer, and gathers her provision in the harvest." Statistics tell us that the "harvest" years for most of us are between the ages of twenty-five and sixty. Therefore it would be wise to lay aside some of the surplus for the latter phase of our lives, when our income abilities decline, so that we don't become a burden to our children.

AVOIDING HOARDING

It's very important to recognize and heed the instruction the Lord gave us with the parable of the so-called rich fool:

> *The land of a certain rich man was very productive. And he began reasoning to himself, saying, "What shall I do, since I have no place to store my crops?" And he said, "This is what I will do: I will tear down my barns and build larger ones, and there I will store all my grain and my goods. And I will say to my soul, 'Soul, you have many goods laid up for many years to come; take your ease, eat, drink and be merry.'" But God said to him, "You fool! This very night your soul is required of you; and now who will own what you have prepared?" So is the man who lays up treasure for himself, and is not rich toward God (Luke 12:16-21).*

There are those Christians who have planned *too* well for retirement. They have enough stored for at least three lifetimes already, and they continue to store even more. Funds that could be used today to feed starving children or bring the gospel to the lost are instead diverted into a retirement account simply because it's a good tax shelter! Again, there is nothing wrong with retirement planning, but hoarding (under any guise) will be judged by God.

KEEP THE RIGHT PRIORITIES

It is interesting to note the outcome of a recent study done by Harvard University. The study involved two groups of Harvard graduates between the ages of sixty-five and seventy-five. One group of 100 men retired at age sixty-five and the other group of 100 continued to work to age seventy-five. In the first group—those who had retired at sixty-five—seven out of eight were dead by age seventy-five. In the second group—men who continued to work—only one in eight had died. The conclusion of this study was that retiring too early in life significantly reduces one's longevity.

If your goal for retirement is a life of ease, heed the warning that study provides. If your retirement goal is to continue a life of service to the Lord, perhaps unencumbered by the need for a large or steady salary, then more power to you. As Christian businessman and leader R. G. LeTourneau once said to his long-time friend Dr. Robert Barnhouse, "Maybe I will retire someday, but I'm just too busy right now." He was about eighty years old at the time!

Jesus says:

> *For this reason you be ready too; for the Son of Man is coming at an hour when you do not think He will. Who then is the faithful and sensible slave whom his master put in charge of his household to give them their food at the proper time? Blessed is that slave whom his master finds so doing when he comes (Matthew 24:44-46).*

A MATTER OF TRUST

David recalls the faithfulness of God to His children:

> *I have been young and now I am old; yet I have not seen the righteous forsaken, or his descendants begging bread (Psalm 37:25).*

Jesus exhorts us to make sure our dependence is upon God and not on the things of this world:

11

For this reason I say to you, do not be anxious for your life, as to what you shall eat, or what you shall drink; nor for your body, as to what you shall put on. Is not life more than food, and the body than clothing?

Look at the birds of the air, that they do not sow, neither do they reap, nor gather into barns, and yet your heavenly Father feeds them. Are you not worth much more than they?

And which of you by being anxious can add a single cubit to his life's span? And why are you anxious about clothing? Observe how the lilies of the field grow; they do not toil nor do they spin, yet I say to you that even Solomon in all his glory did not clothe himself like one of these.

But if God so arrays the grass of the field, which is alive today and tomorrow is thrown into the furnace, will He not much more do so for you, O men of little faith?

Do not be anxious then, saying, "What shall we eat?" or "What shall we drink?" or "With what shall we clothe ourselves?" For all these things the Gentiles eagerly seek; for your heavenly Father knows that you need all these things.

But seek first His kingdom and His righteousness; and all these things shall be added to you. Therefore, do not be anxious for tomorrow; for to-

morrow will care for itself. Each day has enough trouble of its own (Matthew 6:25-34).

In summary, retirement as we know it is a relatively new practice. Few people just two or three generations ago believed it was necessary to stop all activity simply because one was sixty-two or sixty-five years old. Most likely we will return to that same philosophy when most of our modern day programs prove to be unsatisfactory and inadequate. That does not mean that you cannot plan toward a less productive period of advanced age, but it does mean that your plans should be compatible with God's purpose for you at age sixty-five and beyond.

Social Security and Retirement

Decades after it came into being, the name Social Security has become so synonymous with retirement that one seems almost unimaginable without the other.

Millions of Baby Boomers looking forward to retirement are betting their hopes and dreams on Social Security, but will it be there when they need it most? Opinions about the future of the program are varied, but even if it's alive and well in the next twenty to thirty years, some retirees will find it still isn't enough.

Gordon Sherman, head of Social Security's Atlanta Region, says the program is not intended to replace all the income a person would have made if he or she had continued working. For that reason, investments such as IRAs and annuities are needed.

But some would advise against total dependence on Social Security for another reason—what they view as the questionable future of the program.

The debate stems from the way that program funds are being invested. At present, billions of dollars in reserve funds—over and above what Social Security has to pay out each month—are being used to purchase government treasury bills. These bills pay the market rate of interest, and when they come due, the government will be obligated to pay them back to Social Security. These investment returns will then be used to make payments to the large number of Baby Boomers who'll be retiring around the year 2025.

However, some are questioning the logic of investing in a government whose official debt exceeds $2 trillion. In a study for The Heritage Foundation, a Washington think tank, Peter Ferrara noted that Social Security trust funds are not bank accounts in which surpluses pile up, as some might imagine.

"The trust funds are nothing more than a statement of the legal authority Social Security has to draw from U.S. Treasury general revenues," said Ferrara, an associate professor at George Mason Law School. "There is no real money sitting in an account.

"The trust funds 'loan' their annual surpluses to the federal government, which then immediately spends them on other programs. In return, the Social Security trust funds receive new, specially issued federal bonds. These trust funds actually are part of the gross national debt, which grows as the trust funds grow."

At the end of 1991, the trust fund total had risen to $297 billion. The funds are currently growing at nearly $6 billion a month and are projected to reach $369 billion by the end of this year. By the year 2025, the fund will grow to a projected $9.2 trillion.

Ferrara notes that interest on the trust fund bonds has been hailed by some as "income" that the government can use to reduce the budget deficit and pay off the national debt. He points out, however, that the trust funds contain only federal government bonds, and as a result, the interest they earn is a federal government expenditure as well as federal government income.

"In the entire federal budget," he says, "interest 'earned' by the Social Security trust fund does not reduce the federal deficit, but is canceled out as an intra-governmental transfer. It is what economists call a 'wash'; to non-economists, it is the equivalent of an individual transferring his money from one pocket to another."

With this in mind, should the trust funds be invested in something other than government T-bills, such as the private sector? Sherman notes that this option is periodically discussed. But in the past the rationale has been that such investments would not be good for the economy. "With billions and billions of dollars invested," he says, "it wouldn't be long before the federal government would be controlling some corporations." According to Sherman, the possibility of such control has not been a popular idea with corporations and citizens.

One possible investment is public bonds for projects such as roads, but no action has been taken on this alternative.

In the meantime, Social Security trust funds continue to build up billions of dollars' worth of obligations in government T-bills. In Ferrara's opinion, this is just another "paper claim" against the government that will have to be financed out of federal revenues or borrowing when it's cashed in by Social Security.

The huge surplus expected in the year 2025, he says, is nothing more than an additional $9.2 trillion claim against federal taxpayers, in addition to their payroll tax liability.

In Sherman's opinion, the future of Social Security is very secure. Government T-bills, he says, are the "soundest investment we have in this country and the world today."

Sherman also points out that the Japanese and Germans are buying less T-bills than in the past, reducing the amount owed to these two countries. In addition, he says the nation's debt as a percent of its gross domestic product is probably as low as it's ever been.

Other positive signs noted by Sherman are an increase in the nation's birthrate, which had fallen to around 1.7 children per couple. Around 2.1 births per married couple are required to replace the population, creating more workers to pay into Social Security. Sherman says the rate is now 1.9 to 2, which is almost at the replacement level.

When Social Security began in 1935, there were 17 contributors for every person receiving benefits. That number has now fallen to 7 and could drop to 4 by the year 2000. By 2015, it will fall to a projected 2.5 contributors. Low birth rates (affected by abortions) since the early 1960s are to blame for this decrease.

Sherman is also optimistic about what appears to be a growing number of people working past retirement age and therefore continuing to pay into Social Security. Premier corporations, he says, are beginning to recognize the value of these older workers.

In addition, Sherman says, Congress has liberalized guidelines for work after retirement age, allowing individuals to have unlimited earnings and still draw full Social Security benefits at age seventy. He says proposals allowing recipients to have unlimited earnings at sixty-five come up from time to time in Congress. Many believe this would encourage people to continue working and contributing to Social Security after retirement age.

On the other side of the issue, Ferrara is less optimistic about the future of Social Security. Instead of large surpluses in the next century, he sees deficits and resulting Social Security tax increases. As an alternative, he believes workers and their employees should be allowed the choice of substituting private savings and insurance accounts for future Social Security benefits.

"This could reduce reliance on Social Security in the future sufficiently to avoid the need for any tax increases, and even possibly create sufficient room for further payroll tax relief," he says. "Such long-term reform would modernize and liberalize the current Social Security system, allowing workers more freedom of choice and flexibility, greater control over their own resources, broader opportunity to participate in the economy as investors and owners, and the chance for a better deal in the private sector than currently offered to them by the outdated Social Security system."

I would like to offer one additional thought:

Dissolve all federal retirement plans, including those in Congress, and merge them under the Social Security system.

I suspect politicians would be a lot more cautious about how the funds are used if their futures were dependent on Social Security too.

Answers to Questions About Retirement

Given my current wages and my earnings history, I don't think I could ever retire. How can I wisely plan for my later years?

Probably the majority of Christians find themselves in this situation. They simply need to acclimate themselves to the idea that they will be earning a living for the rest of their lives. If this is your situation, you need to plan your career by stages. The first stage would be to work with the goal of being totally debt free, including your home mortgage, by the time you reach a given age (around age fifty or fifty-five). Once your children are grown, you should seek retraining in a skill area that requires less physical strength, such as programming, accounting, art, or woodworking. These skills can successfully carry you throughout your lifetime.

Also, if you are the primary wage earner in your family, you should carry adequate life insurance to provide for your spouse in the event of your death.

I'm in my mid-fifties and can free about $100 a month to put toward retirement. Would I be better off to invest it in an IRA or use it to accelerate my home mortgage?

Assuming that you have adequate savings for current budget needs, I would always recommend paying off the mortgage. Eliminating your mortgage and then using the funds you were paying each month to invest seems a lot more logical. That way you own your home no matter what, and your retirement income needs decrease by the amount of your payments.

However, if you can't eliminate the mortgage before retirement, and you plan to sell your home after retiring, it may make more sense not to pay off your existing mortgage. If your mortgage is an older fixed rate, assumable loan, it can be a real asset in attracting a potential buyer.

Where should I invest my IRA monies?

Follow Solomon's principle:

Divide your portion to seven, or even to eight, for you do not know what misfortune may occur on the earth (Ecclesiastes 11:2).

In other words, don't put all your eggs in one basket—diversify your funds over several types of investments (e.g., CDs, mutual funds, or government securities).

What is your opinion of IRAs as a retirement investment?

My personal opinion about IRAs is that they are excellent tax shelters. In the past, IRAs have gained an additional flexibility, because many banks and other institutions will allow you to take out a self-directed IRA, which is one where you determine where the money will be invested, at least within reasonable parameters.

My only real objection to an IRA is that, in my opinion, they will eventually be used to feed more money into the Social Security system. Because the IRAs are held in cash, or nearly cash accounts, like treasury bills, certificates of deposit, stocks and bonds, and other kinds of paper assets, they can easily be converted if and when the government needs money to feed the Social Security system. I believe that is precisely why the IRA was created and how it will eventually be used. Again, let me restate that this is an opinion and only an opinion.

If there is no other retirement plan available to you, such as a tax-sheltered annuity, a pension and profit-sharing plan, or an HR-10, the IRA is a good alternative. I personally have an IRA plan because it does help in sheltering income and is allowed to accumulate tax-free. Thus it's a good savings plan, as well as an eventual supplement to your own Social Security. (Be sure to consult the new tax laws.)

If I'm wrong about IRAs being absorbed into Social Security, then we'll all benefit; if I'm right, then there's really nothing in particular we can do about it at this time. I encourage you to pray about putting money into an IRA, and if both husband and wife have peace about it, do it.

An alternative to an IRA would be one of the following: (1) invest in collectibles, such as coins, but be sure to seek the counsel of an investment adviser first; or (2) set aside at least 5 percent of your take-home pay (after tithes and taxes) for retirement. When you've accumulated $1,000, begin to invest in a reliable area of the economy, such as rental property. Continue to set aside this amount on a monthly basis and invest it.

> *There is precious treasure and oil in the dwelling of the wise, but a foolish man swallows it up (Proverbs 21:20).*

I have a company pension plan. Should I have other retirement plans as well?

Unfortunately, many companies borrow heavily from their pension funds. The risk is that if the company goes broke, and many do, those funds are lost. You would be wise to take advantage of other investment opportunities such as IRAs in addition to your pension plan.

Both my wife and I are approaching retirement age. Our primary income will be Social Security. With all the publicity about how underfunded the system is, how secure is Social Security?

The best that anyone can do is offer an opinion on the solvency of the

Social Security system. In my opinion, those who are already drawing benefits will be protected to the extent of our government's capability.

The potential difficulties they may face are twofold: First, inflation can easily destroy the value of any fixed income retirement plan. Social Security has a cost-of-living adjuster built into it, but any prolonged inflationary cycle would almost certainly require this to be modified. The government simply lacks the funds to override double digit inflation. Second, the trend in Congress is toward shifting costs such as Medicare to the recipients and taxing benefits at some future date. Either of these can create havoc when you're living on a minimal income.

In your case, since both you and your wife will be drawing retirement benefits, if one of you should die, the survivor may be faced with inadequate income to meet needs. I would encourage you to work at least part-time and develop a savings plan that can eventually provide additional income outside of Social Security.

I've just retired and have qualified for Medicare, but I've been inundated with offers to buy Medicare supplement in-

surance. The costs range from a low of $50 to several hundred dollars a month. Do we need supplemental insurance?

You'll need to weigh the cost of the insurance against the potential liability to evaluate its worth. But, in general, the supplemental insurance protects against catastrophic medical expenses that can wipe out your finances. By the time a Medicare recipient pays the nonreimbursed costs, expenses can amount to many thousands of dollars. In addition, many doctors are refusing to accept direct Medicare payments because they disagree with the fees Medicare assigns. This makes the patient liable to pay in advance and assume responsibility for the charges above those reimbursed by Medicare. I would recommend a policy that covers all charges above that which Medicare reimburses. The cost may seem high, but not when compared to losing all that you have worked for.

I recently retired from the military and have taken a civilian job in Florida, where we eventually plan to retire. Should we buy a home and mortgage it, or wait until we are able to pay cash (about ten years or so from now)?

As a general rule, I would recommend that, after you settle into your job, go ahead and buy a home, even if you have to use a mortgage to do so. Unless we have a general economic slowdown or depression, homes in Florida probably won't depreciate and, in fact, should increase at a fairly steady rate. I would advise that you accelerate the mortgage payments to retire the debt as rapidly as possible and don't sign surety on the note.

I believe one of the essential foundation blocks of a biblically oriented financial plan is a debt-free home. This should be the goal of all Christians, but particularly so for retirees. Personally, I would buy a mobile home if that's what it takes to become debt-free at age sixty-five or older.

My parents are both retired and in their seventies. They are in good health now, but obviously at their age this could change quickly. They live on Social Security and have a little savings. How can we help them prepare for the expenses of nursing home care?

You may not appreciate my initial response to your question, but I don't believe God intended for Christians to shuffle their parents off to nursing homes, regardless of what society promotes. There may be exceptions based on unique medical conditions, but we have made the exceptions the rule today. I believe Christians of our generation need to take a refresher course on honoring their fathers and mothers.

For those who have medical needs that necessitate nursing home care, only a few alternatives are available. One is an insurance policy for nursing home care. A few companies offer such policies, but the restrictions on age and health are severe, and the costs are very high.

Another alternative is government welfare. Once elderly patients have exhausted all available resources, they usually qualify for state and federal welfare assistance. Let me say here that many otherwise honest Christians have misused this privilege by transferring assets from an elderly relative to other people to qualify for indigent care. This is wrong, and to do so willfully is a sin.

> *But your iniquities have made a separation between you and your God, and your sins have hidden His face from you, so that He does not hear (Isaiah 59:2).*

Social Security Benefits

WHO IS COVERED?

Social Security earnings are credited to a person's account based on a "quarter of coverage" system. Before 1978, workers earned a quarter of coverage if they were paid $50 or more in a calendar quarter. The amount is determined at the end of each year and has increased annually to keep pace with average wages. The requirement for 1991 was $540 of earnings per calendar quarter.

FULLY INSURED

"Fully insured" is a status you reach after accumulating forty quarters of coverage. A person employed for at least ten years in jobs covered by Social Security can normally assume to be fully insured. Being fully insured means you are entitled to full benefits.

CURRENTLY INSURED

"Currently insured" is a status you achieve after accumulating at least six (6) quarters of coverage in the thirteen-quarter period ending with the quarter in which you die or become disabled. Generally, a currently insured person may be entitled to disability benefits but not retirement benefits.

RETIREMENT BENEFITS

To qualify for retirement benefits you must be at least sixty-two years old and fully insured. Generally, if one spouse is receiving old-age benefits, the other spouse is also entitled to benefits upon reaching age sixty-two. A spouse is eligible for benefits before age sixty-two if he or she is caring for a child who is entitled to receive benefits.

If you wait until age sixty-five before applying for old-age benefits, you're entitled to receive the full amount (100 percent) of your entitlement. This full entitlement is called your "Primary Insurance Account" (PIA). However, you can apply for a reduced amount of benefits at age sixty-two.

If you claim retirement benefits before age sixty-five, the amount of your monthly benefit is permanently reduced by certain percentages, depending upon your age when the benefits are claimed. If the benefits start at exactly age sixty-two, the reduction is about 20 percent of your full Primary Insurance Account (PIA). For each month you wait after reaching age sixty-two, a formula is used to determine your benefit amount. If you continue working past the full-benefit age of sixty-five and are not receiving benefit payments, monthly benefits are increased by 3 percent for each year after you reach age sixty-five.

When you receive retirement benefits, your children under the age of eighteen are also eligible for benefits if they're single and living at home. A child's benefits are usually discontinued upon reaching age eighteen (age twenty-two if a full-time student, but these student benefits are scheduled to be phased out).

A mother's benefit payments based on her having a child in her care will normally stop when that child reaches age sixteen (unless the child is disabled) even though the child is a full-time student and receives benefit payment in his or her own right until age eighteen.

DISABILITY BENEFITS

When you qualify as being a disabled worker, you're entitled to receive monthly benefit payments in the same amount you would have been paid had you been retired under normal conditions. Meeting the requirements for disability benefits is not easy, but there are exceptions for persons disabled before reaching age thirty-one and for the blind. To qualify as disabled, you must meet all of the following conditions:

1. Be under the age of sixty-five and have enough Social Security coverage when the waiting period for disability benefits begin. At present there is a five-month waiting period, and payments start in the sixth full month of disability; and

2. The degree of your disability must be severe enough to prevent you from doing any substantial gainful work; and

3. The disability must last (or be expected to last) for at least twelve months or to result in death; and

4. You must have accumulated at least twenty quarters of coverage under the system in the forty-quarter period that ends in the quarter you became disabled.

Disability benefits may also be paid to disabled children past the age of twenty-two if they were disabled before reaching age twenty-two and have remained disabled. Persons entitled to disability benefits for twenty-four straight months also qualify for Medicare benefits.

SURVIVOR BENEFITS

When a person covered by Social Security dies, monthly benefits may be payable to certain survivors. The amounts paid are based on the person's full Social Security entitlement (full PIA), even though the person started receiving benefits before reaching age sixty-five.

For a fully-insured worker, survivor benefits are payable to a widow or widower, or surviving divorced wife or husband, age sixty or over (ages fifty to fifty-nine if disabled), as well as to the worker's dependent parents who are age sixty-two or over.

Benefits paid to a surviving spouse because he or she cares for a child will be discontinued when the child reaches age eighteen, even if the child is a full-time student receiving benefit payments in his or her own right.

LUMP-SUM DEATH BENEFIT PAYMENTS

When a fully- or currently-insured worker dies, a one-time lump-sum death benefit of $225 is payable to his or her surviving spouse if that spouse is eligible for (or would be eligible except for age) monthly survivor's benefits. If there is no eligible surviving spouse, the lump-sum death benefit can be paid to a surviving child who is eligible for child's benefits.

MEDICARE BENEFITS

Medicare is a two-part insurance program covering the hospital and medical care costs for persons age sixty-five or older who are entitled to receive Social Security. Part A covers hospital insurance benefits, and Part B covers medical insurance benefits.

APPLYING FOR SOCIAL SECURITY

Your Social Security benefits are not automatically started when you become eligible to receive them. You must apply for each benefit to which you are entitled. Since it takes time to process the paperwork, you should apply for benefits at least three months before your actual entitlement date.

When applying for benefits, you'll need to have your Social Security card (or proof of your number) and be able to prove your age with either a birth or baptismal certificate. A copy of your marriage license is necessary when applying for survival or spousal benefits. When applying for child's benefits, you'll need a copy of his or her birth certificate.

Veterans' Benefits

Generally, to qualify for VA benefits, a veteran's active duty service must have been terminated under conditions other than dishonorable. While an honorable or general discharge will qualify a veteran for most benefits, a dishonorable discharge usually disqualifies a veteran for most benefits. A bad conduct discharge may enable the veteran to qualify for some benefits, depending on the VA's determination of facts surrounding the member's discharge.

SURVIVOR'S AND DEPENDENTS' EDUCATION

If a veteran dies or is permanently and totally disabled as a result of military service, his or her surviving spouse and dependent children may qualify to receive financial help for educational purposes. These benefits are also available to a spouse and dependent children of a member who is a prisoner of war or is missing in action for more than ninety days.

Training can be in an approved vocational school, business school, college, professional school, or an apprentice or on-the-job training program. It also includes training in a secondary school, by correspondence, or in an educational institution offering farm co-op programs.

Normally the length of training cannot exceed forty-five months of school or the equivalent of forty-five months if enrolled on a part-time basis. A child's marital status is no barrier to receiving these benefits, but the remarriage of a surviving spouse will end his or her entitlement unless the new marriage is terminated by death or divorce.

DEPENDENCY AND INDEMNITY BENEFITS

The payment of Dependency and Indemnity Compensation (DIC) was originally intended to assist the surviving spouse and dependent children of a veteran whose death resulted from a service-connected disability or cause. Changes in the new law have broadened the scope of DIC benefits to include the survivors of certain veterans whose deaths do not meet the earlier (and more stringent) rules.

WHEN DEATH IS DUE TO A NON-SERVICE-CONNECTED CAUSE

DIC payments can be authorized to certain survivors of veterans who were totally disabled from a service-connected cause but whose deaths were not the result of that service-connected cause or disability. Benefits are payable if the veteran was continuously rated as totally disabled for a period of ten or more years or, if so rated for less than ten years, was so rated for at least five years from the date he or she was discharged.

Benefit payments are authorized for the veteran's surviving spouse, to any unmarried children under the age of eighteen (under twenty-three if they are students), and to certain helpless children.

DEATH PENSION FOR SURVIVING SPOUSES

Based on financial need and ability to qualify, a veteran's surviving spouse and unmarried children under eighteen (under twenty-three if students) may be entitled to a monthly VA pension.

For the survivors to qualify, the deceased veteran must have had at least ninety days of service and must have been separated or discharged under conditions other than dishonorable—unless the separation was due to a service-connected disability. If the veteran died while serving on active duty, but the death was not in the line of duty, benefits may be payable if he or she had completed at least two years of honorable active military service.

Insofar as the surviving spouse is concerned, he or she must have married the veteran at least one year prior to death unless a child resulted from the marriage.

VA BURIAL BENEFITS

The Veterans Administration will furnish a headstone or marker to memorialize or mark the grave of a veteran buried in a national, state, or private cemetery. The VA also provides markers to eligible family members interred in a national or state veterans' cemetery.

If death is not service-connected, the VA provides a burial allowance of

$300 if the veteran was entitled at the time of death to VA compensation or died in a VA medical facility. A plot or interment allowance of $150 is also available if the veteran is entitled to the burial allowance, served during a war period, or was discharged or retired from service because of a disability that was incurred or aggravated in the line of duty. A veteran buried in a national or other federal cemetery, however, is not eligible for this plot allowance. The plot allowance may be paid to a state if the veteran was buried in a state veterans' cemetery.

If the death is service-connected, the VA will pay an amount not to exceed $1,000 in lieu of the burial and plot allowance. The VA will also provide an American flag for use in covering a casket, and a reimbursement for part of the cost of a private headstone or marker bought after the veteran's death. (The amount was $71 as of 1990.)

For further information, contact the Veterans Administration, 810 Vermont Avenue (40) NW, Washington, DC 20420.

Determining Insurance Needs

How Much Insurance Do
I Need and Can I Afford?

The amount of life insurance a family needs depends on many variables such as family income, ages of the children, ability of the wife to earn an income, Social Security status, the standard of living you hope to provide, and outstanding debts.

Present Income Per Year

How much income is being provided by the breadwinner of the family? The goal is to provide for the family so that they may continue the same living standard they enjoy under this income.

Payments No Longer Required

Family expenses should drop as a result of the death of the breadwinner. For example, a second car may no longer be required; less income (or different income) will mean less taxes; activities or hobbies would not be an expense; investments or savings may be reduced or stopped.

INCOME AVAILABLE

The breadwinner's death may initiate income from some other sources. Social Security income will depend on one's eligibility, which in turn is determined by the time in the system, amount of earnings, and ages of spouse and dependent children. Income may also be available from retirement plans, investments, annuities, and the like.

The income-earning potential of the wife is a definite asset to the family. Ages of the children are a factor here. A minimum insurance program should provide time for obtaining or sharpening job skills if necessary.

ADDITIONAL INCOME REQUIRED TO SUPPORT FAMILY

The income presently being earned, less the payments no longer required, and less the income available results in the income that needs to be supplied in order for the family to continue living on the same level enjoyed through the income of the husband.

INSURANCE REQUIRED TO PROVIDE NEEDED INCOME

If provision could be made in an "ideal" manner, the insurance money invested at 10 percent would return the needed amount of income to the family. To find the required amount of insurance, multiply the income required to support the family by 10.

Example: $7,000 additional income is required to support the family; $7,000 x 10 equals $70,000. If you then invest this amount, $70,000 in insurance invested at 10 percent would provide the needed funds.

LUMP SUM REQUIREMENTS

In addition to the insurance required to produce the regular sustained income, lump sums may be required for specific purposes (e.g., college education). Those needs should be determined and added to the total amount of insurance.

Are funds needed to pay off the home mortgage? This should be discussed as a part of the family plan. If mortgage payments are being made under the existing income, then this could be continued under the sustained income provision. Since paying for the home would significantly boost the insurance requirement, this will also raise the amount that must be spent for insurance.

ASSETS AVAILABLE

Determine the assets that are available for family provision. Subtract this amount from the desired amount of insurance.

Equity in a home can be counted as an asset only if the survivors plan to sell it.

TOTAL INSURANCE NEEDED

The total tells how much insurance is needed. This must be balanced against how much can be spent for insurance. If the insurance dollars are limited, it will be necessary to get as close to the plan as possible with those dollars. Term insurance with its lower initial premiums probably offers the best opportunity for adequate provision with the fewest dollars.

The plan should also include instructions as to how the insurance money is to be used.

NOTE: Insurance needs should be reviewed periodically. Family changes (i.e., new additions, children becoming employed or leaving home, inflation changes, income changes, and the like) should prompt an insurance review.

Estate Taxes

FEDERAL DEATH TAXES

Although the federal estate tax code has been greatly improved over the last decade, poor planning can still result in some significant tax liabilities. The current federal estate tax ranges from 37 percent to 60 percent. But for the majority of estates this will represent no real liability since the tax begins with estates that have a net worth of $600,000 or more. Also, all assets left to a surviving spouse are exempt from any tax.

The greatest potential tax liability usually involves estates where both spouses die in a short time frame or where there is no surviving spouse. In these instances the estate will be composed of all assets in which the deceased had any interest, including real properties, insurance, revocable trusts, pension-profit sharings, assets, and the like.

Gifts made in excess of the gift tax exemption of $10,000 per year per person, or $20,000 for a couple, are also potentially taxable in the estate. In addition, the courts have traditionally held that all gifts made within three years of death can be included in the final estate evaluation if such gifts are deemed to have been made in contemplation of death. Generally the evidence to the contrary consists of an established pattern of giving in previous years.

After the amount of the estate (or gift) has been reduced by the various authorized deductions or exclusions, the amount of tax can be tentatively determined by using the rates in the United Rate Schedule for Estates and Gift Taxes. Your authorized tax credit is then applied, further reducing the taxable amount.

Of course, determining the actual amount of taxes owed is often complicated, and it's a good idea to let a professional financial planner or tax accountant help reduce the tax liability of your estate as much as possible.

STATE DEATH TAXES

When most people think about taxes that are taken out of an estate, they typically think about estate taxes. In reality, only eighteen states now have estate taxes. The others use a combination of either death taxes or pick-up taxes.

The amount each state can collect from an estate varies widely, with some states taking only the deductible amount allowed from the federal inheritance tax. This last category is called "pick-up" tax since it is the amount picked up from the federal taxes and represents no additional cost to the heirs.

The federal estate tax code exempts all assets left to a surviving spouse and $600,000 in assets left to all other beneficiaries. However, that same exemption does not always apply to the taxes levied by a state. As of 1990, several states still levy a tax on spousal inheritance.

The amount an estate will be required to pay in state death or inheritance taxes can affect the heirs significantly since the taxes must be paid in cash. Sometimes it is economically beneficial to relocate your primary residence in light of the potential taxes due. You can obtain a current quotation of the taxes levied by your state by writing the state's tax commissioner's office.

Widows Need Early Financial Training

As of 1990, the average age at which a woman is widowed is fifty-two. Statistically, about 82 percent of all married women will be widowed at least once in their lifetimes. After I mentioned these statistics at a conference not long ago, one of the male attendees asked, "Does that mean if I divorce my wife at fifty-one, that I will live longer?" No, it doesn't work that way. But what it does mean is that a wise man (wise with the wisdom of God) will train his wife to be his successor, since he knows the chances are he will predecease her.

Most people, Christians included, don't like to discuss death, and so they delay talking about it until it's too late. But if more women in the church who are widowed would speak up about some of their problems, other women would probably feel more motivated to deal with the possibility of being widowed.

The husbands who die don't always die of natural causes. In our mobile society, it is common for a man to die by accident. In my counseling with widows, I found nearly half of all those I counseled had lost husbands to accidents. Following are two examples from my counseling. The names are changed, for obvious reasons, but the people are real; so are the problems.

Nate and Sherri Long had come in for budget counseling after attending a seminar at their church. They had been going into debt a little more each year and were determined to get their finances under control. Their problem was mostly related to vacations, overruns, and two fairly new automobiles, each with sizable payments. They put the newest car up for sale, intending to use the proceeds to retire all their credit card debt and eliminate one car note. They never made it.

Nate was returning from a business trip and caught a Southern Airways flight out of Memphis to Atlanta. On the way, the plane ran into some bad weather and, due to an apparent error on the part of a flight controller, the pilot was routed directly into the path of a severe thunderstorm. Sixty-three passengers lost their lives, including Nate Long. Suddenly Sherri found herself a widow at the age of thirty-two.

Around the same time Nate and Sherri came for help, another couple, Allen and Nancy, had also come in for counseling. Allen was a successful architect on contract with the federal government. Their income was about $100,000 annually but, because of a series of bad investments, they owed nearly $75,000 in unsecured bank loans. They also lived in a home that consumed more than half of Allen's salary, and they drove two leased and very expensive, imported cars. The net result was that Nancy had to go to work just to provide enough income for basic necessities.

Like Nate Long, Allen was flying in the plane from Memphis to Atlanta and was killed. Over the next two years I had a chance to work with other advisers helping both Sherri and Nancy. Their stories are examples of what good and poor planning can do.

Once the shock of Nate's death wore off and the funeral was completed, Sherri called to ask for an appointment. Nate had taken the time to prepare a will, and in one note-book he had assembled all their insurance policies, their agent's name and address, the name of their family attorney, and all the information necessary to file for Social Security survivor's benefits, as well as his veteran's benefits. In one two-hour session we had completed all the required forms and had them ready to mail.

A settlement from the airlines and the Federal Aviation Administration was pending, but it was tied up in court for the next four years. However, with her budget well established and enough money coming in from Social Security and workman's compensation (awarded because Nate was killed while on business for his employer), Sherri had no abnormal financial pressures.

On the other hand, Nancy's situation went from bad to worse. Allen left no will, and although Nancy was assured a portion of the estate by state law, she could receive as little as a child's share. With the large settlement from the airlines and FAA pending, the judge was not willing to assign her more than the legal limit. Potential heirs filed petitions with the court, and Nancy was forced to hire attorneys to protect her interests. Since Allen worked for the government, he had no Social Security benefits available. The government did continue his salary without interruption, but after six months they threatened to sue Nancy for recovery of the funds, saying her compensation should have been paid by workman's compensation. The sum that workman's compensation would have paid was substantially less than Allen's salary, so Nancy was facing another lawsuit, in addition to those filed by her husband's creditors.

By the time the court case was settled, both widows received a settlement of nearly $1 million. Sherri was able to give a substantial portion of hers to her church, set up a college trust fund for her children, and invest the rest to provide a comfortable income.

Nancy paid 40 percent of her settlement in attorneys' fees. Creditors took another $200,000, and the government settled for $40,000 in back pay. Obviously, she still had enough to live on, but almost immediately she invested a substantial portion with a friend from her church and lost nearly $200,000 over the next two years. In the end she was forced into the job market to support herself and her two children. I attribute much of her troubles to Allen's lack of planning and her lack of adequate training.

You may not believe any of this will ever happen to you, but it can! Your circumstance can change literally overnight. Therefore, one of the the best decisions husbands and wives will ever make is to ensure that the wife knows how to manage money properly.

The single most important decision that any recent widow will make is to make *no* decisions concerning investments, loans, new cars, or anything else that might jeopardize your assets, for at least one year. That is the time when a widow is the most vulnerable and therefore susceptible to bad advice or outright fraud. The first year should be spent getting adjusted to your new life and educated on the ins and outs of money management.

Other Materials by Larry Burkett:

Books in This series:
Financial Freedom
Sound Investments
Major Purchases
Insurance Plans
Giving and Tithing
Personal Finances
Surviving the 90's Economy
Your Financial Future

Other Books:
The Coming Economic Earthquake
Debt-Free Living
Financial Planning Workbook
How to Manage Your Money
Using Your Money Wisely
Your Finances in Changing Times
New Book on Retirement Planning
(hardcover release coming
in October 1992)

Videos:
Your Finances in Changing Times
Two Masters
How to Manage Your Money
The Financial Planning Workbook

Other Resources:
Financial Planning Organizer
Debt-Free Living Cassette